YO MOMMA JOKES FOR KIDS

YO

MOMMA'S

SO

FAT...

Yo momma's so fat, that she went on a light diet. As soon as it's light she starts eating.

Yo momma's so fat, that she can't even jump to a conclusion.

Yo momma's so fat, that when she takes a shower, her feet don't get wet.

Yo momma's so fat, that when she went to SeaWorld the whales started singing "We Are Family"!

Yo momma's so fat, that she has smaller fat women orbiting around her!

Yo momma's so fat, that she expresses her weight in scientific notation.

Yo momma's so fat, that when she fell over she rocked herself asleep trying to get up again.

Yo momma's so fat, that that when she sits on the beach, Greenpeace shows up and tries to tow her back into the ocean.

Yo momma's so fat, that I had to take a train and two buses just to get on her good side!

Yo momma's so fat, that went she stepped in the water, Thailand had to declare another tsunami warning.

Yo momma's so fat, that eating contests have banned her because she is unfair competition.

Yo momma's so fat, that her pictures had to be aerial views!

Yo momma's so fat, that when she wants to shake someone's hand, she has to give directions!

Yo momma's so fat, that they have to grease the bath tub to get her out!

Yo momma's so fat, that when she goes to a restaurant she looks at the menu and says, "Okay!"

Yo momma's so fat, that she can fall from both sides of the bed at the same time.

Yo momma's so fat she's got more nooks and crannies than an English muffin.

Yo momma's so fat, that when she plays hopscotch, she goes New York, Chicago, and Los Angeles.

Yo momma's so fat, she gave Dracula diabetes.

Yo momma's so fat, that when she gets in an elevator, it has to go down.

Yo momma's so fat, that she uses redwoods to pick her teeth.

Yo momma's so fat, that she has been declared a natural habitat.

Yo momma's so fat, that they use the elastic in her underwear for bungee jumping.

Yo momma's so fat, that her baby pictures were taken by satellite.

Yo momma's so fat, that Sarah Palin can see her from her house.

Yo momma's so fat, that the last time the landlord saw her, he doubled the rent.

Yo momma's so fat, she put on her lipstick with a paint-roller!

Yo momma's so fat, that when you climb on her shoulders your ears pop.

Yo momma's so fat, that even Dora can't explore her!

Yo momma's so fat, that when she turns around people throw her a welcome back party.

Yo momma's so fat, that when she skips breakfast, Kellogg's goes out of business.

Yo momma's so fat, that when she dances at a concert the whole band skips.

Yo momma's so fat, that she has her own gravity field.

Yo momma's so fat, that she took geometry in high school just because she heard there was pi.

Yo momma's so fat, my group photo is still printing.

Yo momma's so fat, that her driver's license picture says, "Continued on other side."

Yo momma's so fat, that when she lies on the beach, people run around yelling, "Free Willy!"

Yo momma's so fat, that the highway patrol made her wear a "Caution! Wide Turn" sign.

Yo momma's so fat, that she walked into the Gap and filled it.

Yo momma's so fat, that when she walked in front of the TV, I missed 3 seasons of The Simpsons.

Yo momma's so fat, that when she talks to herself, it's a long distance call.

Yo momma's so fat, that she was zoned for commercial development.

Yo momma's so fat, that I ran around her twice and got lost.

Yo momma's so fat, her belly button has an echo.

Yo momma's so fat, that when she goes to an amusement park, people try to ride her.

Yo momma's so fat, that when she steps on a scale it says, "One at a time, please."

Yo momma's so fat, that they registered her to vote eight times!

Yo momma's so fat, that when she goes to a buffet, she gets the group rate.

Yo momma's so fat, that her shadow weighs 100 pounds.

Yo momma's so fat, that they had to let out the shower curtain

Yo momma's so fat, that when she wears a yellow raincoat, people yell, "Taxi!"

Yo momma's so fat, that at the zoo, the elephants throw her peanuts.

Yo momma's so fat, she's got her own area code!

Yo momma's so fat, that she when she was floating in the ocean Spain claimed her for the new world.

Yo momma's so fat, that when she sings, it's over for everybody.

Yo momma's so fat, that she puts mayonnaise on her mayonnaise.

Yo momma's so fat, that NASA orbits a satellite around her!

Yo momma's so fat, she's on both sides of the family.

Yo momma's so fat, she has more rolls then the town's bakery.

Yo momma's so fat, that she gets group insurance.

Yo momma's so fat, she went skydiving today and everybody thought it was an eclipse.

Yo momma's so fat, that that when I tried to drive around her I ran out of gas.

Yo momma's so fat, that every time she walks in high heels, she strikes oil!

Yo momma's so fat, Donald Trump placed her as a border wall.

Yo momma's so fat, that she doesn't eat with a fork, she eats with a forklift.

Yo momma's so fat, that she has to buy three airline tickets.

Yo momma's so fat, she had to go to Sea World to get baptized.

Yo momma's so fat, that when God said, "Let there be light!" he told her to move out the way first.

Yo momma's so fat, that she went to the movie theater and sat next to everyone.

Yo momma's so fat, that when we went to the drive-in movies we didn't have to pay for her because we dressed her up as a car.

Yo momma's so fat, she threw on a sheet for Halloween and went as Antarctica.

Yo momma's so fat, she can only take a selfie in panorama mode.

Yo momma's so fat, that in an attempt to beam her up, the ship was pulled down to the surface.

Yo momma's so fat, that her belly button doesn't have lint, it has sweaters.

Yo momma's so fat, that when she fell, no one was laughing but the floor was cracking up.

Yo momma's so fat, that her belly arrives at her house half-an-hour before her.

Yo momma's so fat, that she has to iron her pants on the driveway.

Yo momma's so fat, that when she asked for a waterbed, they put a blanket over the ocean!

Yo momma's so fat, that when she runs the fifty-yard dash she needs an overnight bag.

Yo momma's so fat, that she and the Great Wall of China are used as reference points when astronauts look at the Earth.

Yo momma's so fat, when she goes camping the bears hide their food.

Yo momma's so fat, that her cereal bowl came with a lifeguard.

Yo momma's so fat, that the only exercise she gets is when she chases the ice cream truck.

Yo momma's so fat, she could be classified as a dinosaur.

Yo momma's so fat, that when she sits around the house, she really sits around the house!

Yo momma's so fat, she can't reach her back pocket.

Yo momma's so fat, she sweats chocolate pudding!

Yo momma's so fat, she has to get out of her car to change radio stations.

Yo momma's so fat, that she was born on the fourth, fifth, and sixth of June.

Yo momma's so fat, her blood type is Ragu.

Yo momma's so fat, that when she gets on the scale it says "To be continued."

Yo momma's so fat, that when she lays on the beach no one else gets any sun!

Yo momma's so fat, that when she walks she changes the earth's rotation!

Yo momma's so fat, that when she sat on an iPhone, it turned into an iPad.

Yo momma's so fat, when she takes a selfie it takes up all the phone storage.

Yo momma's so fat, that when she got hit by a car, she had to go to the hospital to have it removed.

Yo momma's so fat, that she gets her toenails painted at Bucky's Auto Body.

Yo momma's so fat, she left the house in high heels and came back she in flip flops.

Yo momma's so fat, she mistakes her scale for a phone number.

Yo momma's so fat, that she comes at you from all directions.

Yo momma's so fat, that she could sell shade.

Yo momma's so fat, that whenever she goes to the beach the tide comes in!

Yo momma's so fat, that when she goes to an all you can eat buffet, they have to install speed bumps.

Yo momma's so fat, she wore a red sweater and all of the kids pointed at her and said, "Hey, Kool-Aid Man!"

Yo momma's so fat, that the sign inside one restaurant says, "Maximum occupancy: 200, or Yo momma."

Yo momma's so fat, her memory foam forgot.

YO

MOMMA'S

SO

HAIRY...

Yo momma's so hairy, that people think they've spotted Bigfoot.

Yo momma's so hairy, that she shaves her legs with a weed wacker.

Yo momma's so hairy, that people run up to her and say "Chewbacca, can I get your autograph?"

Yo momma's so hairy, that if she could fly she'd look like a magic carpet.

Yo momma's so hairy, that she looks like a Chia Pet with a sweater on.

Yo momma's so hairy, that when she's at the beach people think she's wearing a fur coat!

YO

MOMMA'S

SO

OLD...

Yo momma's so old, that she called the cops when David and Goliath started to fight.

Yo momma's so old, that she DJ'd at the Boston Tea Party.

Yo momma's so old, I told, her to act her age she died.

Yo momma's so old, she still owes Moses a quarter!

Yo momma's so old, the movie "Jurassic Park" brought back memories

Yo momma's so old, that when she was born, the Dead Sea just had a small cough.

Yo momma's so old, her memory is in black and white.

Yo momma's so old, her Bible is autographed.

Yo momma's so old, that her birth certificate is written in Roman numerals.

Yo momma's so old, that she drove a chariot to high school.

Yo momma's so old, that she baby-sat for Adam and Eve.

Yo momma's so old, that her candles cost more than her birthday cake.

Yo momma's so old, that she walked into an antique store and they kept her.

Yo momma's so old, that she took her driver's test on a dinosaur.

Yo momma's so old, she remembers when the Mayans published their calendar.

Yo momma's so old, that she learned to write on cave walls.

Yo momma's so old, that when she was in school there was no history class.

Yo momma's so old, that her social security number is 1.

YO

MOMMA'S

SO

POOR...

Yo momma's so poor, that when I ring the doorbell she says, "Ding dong."

Yo momma's so poor, that I went to her house and tore down the cob webs, and she said "Who's ripped down the curtains?"

Yo momma's so poor, that I threw a rock at a trash can and she popped out and said "Who knocked?"

Yo momma's so poor, at the park the ducks throw bread to her.

Yo momma's so poor, that I saw her wrestling a squirrel for a peanut.

Yo momma's so poor, that she went to McDonald's and put a milkshake on layaway.

Yo momma's so poor, that I went through her front door and ended up in her back yard.

Yo momma's so poor, that she watches TV on an Etch-A-Sketch.

Yo momma's so poor, that I came over for dinner and she read me recipes.

Yo momma's so poor, that when I went over to her house for dinner and grabbed a paper plate, she said "Please don't use the good china!"

Yo momma's so poor, that I walked into her house and swatted a firefly and Yo momma said, "Who turned off the lights?"

Yo momma's so poor, that she married just to get the rice!

Yo momma's so poor, that she had to get a second mortgage on her cardboard box.

Yo momma's so poor, that she waves around a Popsicle stick and calls it air conditioning.

Yo momma's so poor, that burglars break in and leave money.

Yo momma's so poor, that she can't even put her two cents in a conversation.

Yo momma's so poor, that she's got more furniture on her porch than in her house.

Yo momma's so poor, that I saw her running after a garbage truck with a shopping list.

Yo momma's so poor, that when I saw her rolling some trash cans around in an alley, I asked her what she was doing, she said, "Remodeling."

Yo momma's so poor, that she got in an elevator and thought it was a mobile home.

Yo momma's so poor, that she washes her paper napkins.

Yo momma's so poor, that she can't even afford to pay attention!

YO

MOMMA'S

SO

SHORT...

Yo momma's so short, that she slam-dunks her bus fare.

Yo momma's so short, she can limbo under the door.

Yo momma's so short, that when she sat on the curb her feet didn't touch the ground.

Yo momma's so short, that she does pull-ups on a staple.

Yo momma's so short, that you can see her feet on her driver's license!

Yo momma's so short, that she models for trophies.

Yo momma's so short, that she has to use a ladder to pick up a dime.

YO

MOMMA'S

SO

SKINNY...

Yo momma's so skinny, that she turned sideways and disappeared.

Yo momma's so skinny, that when she wore her yellow dress, she looked like a pencil.

Yo momma's so skinny, that her pants only have one belt loop.

Yo momma's so skinny, that she hula hoops with a Cheerio.

Yo momma's so skinny, that she can dodge rain drops.

Yo momma's so skinny, that if she turned sideways and stuck out her tongue, she would look like a zipper.

Yo momma's so skinny, that if she had a sesame seed on her head, she'd look like a push pin.

Yo momma's so skinny, that she looks like a mic stand.

Yo momma's so skinny, that you can save her from drowning by tossing her a Fruit Loop.

Yo momma's so skinny, that she can see out a peephole with both eyes.

YO

MOMMA'S

SO

STUPID...

Yo momma's so stupid, that she spent twenty minutes looking at an orange juice box because it said "concentrate".

Yo momma's so stupid, that she asked for a price check at the dollar store.

Yo momma's so stupid, that when she took an IQ test, the results came out negative.

Yo momma's so stupid, that when burglars broke into her apartment and took her TV she ran after them to give them the remote as well.

Yo momma's so stupid, she tripped over a cordless phone

Yo momma's so stupid, that the only reason she opened her email was because she heard there was spam.

Yo momma's so stupid, that she thought Dunkin' Donuts was a basketball team!

Yo momma's so stupid, that that she tried to put M&M's in alphabetical order!

Yo momma's so stupid, she waited for the stop sign to turn green.

Yo momma's so stupid, she got hit by a parked car.

Yo momma's so stupid, that she said, "What's that letter after x?" And I said "Y." And she said "Cause I wanna know!"

Yo momma's so stupid, that she called the 7-11 to see when time they closed.

Yo momma's so stupid, that she went to the dentist to get a Bluetooth.

Yo momma's so stupid, that she got locked in a grocery store and starved!

Yo momma's so stupid, that when she locked her keys in the car, it took her all day to get Yo family out.

Yo momma's so stupid, that she climbed over a glass wall to see what was behind it.

Yo momma's so stupid, that when your dad said it was chilly outside, she ran out the door with a spoon.

Yo momma's so stupid, she thought a quarterback was a refund.

Yo momma's so stupid, that when she went for a blood test, she asked for time to study.

Yo momma's so stupid, that she put 2 quarters in her ears and thought she was listening to 50 cent.

Yo momma's so stupid, that when I asked her why she was walking down the street yelling into an envelope, she said she was sending a voice mail.

Yo momma's so stupid, that she failed a survey.

Yo momma's so stupid, that I told her I was reading a book by Homer and she asked if I had read anything written by Bart.

Yo momma's so stupid, she sold her car to get gasoline money!

Yo momma's so stupid, that when she went to Walgreen's she said "Hey, these walls aren't green!"

Yo momma's so stupid, she brought lipstick to a make-up test.

Yo momma's so stupid, that if she spoke her mind, she'd be speechless.

Yo momma's so stupid, that she ran outside with a purse because she heard there was change in the weather.

Yo momma's so stupid, she walked into an antique shop and asked, "What's new?"

Yo momma's so stupid, that she ordered her sushi well done.

Yo momma's so stupid, that she got fired from the M&M factory for throwing away all the W's.

Yo momma's so stupid, she tried to steal a free sample!

Yo momma's so stupid, that if you gave her a penny for her thoughts, you'd get change.

Yo momma's so stupid, she put on bug spray before going to the flea market.

Yo momma's so stupid, she took the Pepsi challenge and chose Dr. Pepper.

Yo momma's so stupid, that when the judge said "Order in the court," she said, "I'll have a hamburger and a Coke."

Yo momma's so stupid, that she took lessons for a player piano.

Yo momma's so stupid, she used a real mouse to use the computer.

Yo momma's so stupid, that it takes her an hour to cook minute rice.

Yo momma's so stupid, she stepped on a crack and broke her own back.

Yo momma's so stupid, it took her two hours to watch 60 Minutes.

Yo momma's so stupid, that when she asked me what yield meant and I said, "Slow down," she said "What... does.... yield... mean?"

Yo momma's so stupid, that when I asked her if she wanted to play one on one, she said "Ok, but what are the teams?"

Yo momma's so stupid, that she got locked inside a motorcycle.

Yo momma's so stupid, she took a ruler to bed to see how long she slept.

Yo momma's so stupid, she put a quarter in a parking meter and waited for a gumball to come out.

Yo momma's so stupid, she put on a coat to chew winter fresh gum.

Yo momma's so stupid, she had to call the operator to get the number for 911!

Yo momma's so stupid, that she put two M&M's in her ears and thought she was listening to Eminem.

Yo momma's so stupid, that she threw a rock at the ground and missed.

YO

MOMMA'S

SO

UGLY...

Yo momma's so ugly, that she put the Halloween store out of business.

Yo momma's so ugly, that she looks like she's been in a dryer filled with rocks.

Yo momma's so ugly, that when she went to a beautician it took ten hours to get a quote!

Yo momma's so ugly, that that when she sits in the sand on the beach, cats try to bury her.

Yo momma's so ugly, that when she looks in the mirror it says, "Viewer discretion is advised."

Yo momma's so ugly, that she tried to take a bath and the water jumped out!

Yo momma's so ugly, that her face is blurred on her driver's license.

Yo momma's so ugly, that when she walks in the kitchen, the rats jump on the table and start screaming.

Yo momma's so ugly, that just after she was born, her mother said "What a treasure!" and her father said, "Yes, let's go bury it."

Yo momma's so ugly, that she threw a boomerang and it wouldn't come back.

Yo momma's so ugly, that when she looks in the mirror, the reflection looks back and shakes its head.

Yo momma's so ugly, her portraits hang themselves.

Yo momma's so ugly, that a sculpture of her face is used to torture people.

Yo momma's so ugly, that when I took her to a haunted house, and she came out with a job application.

Yo momma's so ugly, yo grandma had to feed her with a sling shot.

Yo momma's so ugly, that she made an onion cry!

Yo momma's so ugly, that that your father takes her to work with him so that he doesn't have to kiss her goodbye.

Yo momma's so ugly, that I took her to the zoo, and the zookeeper said, "Thanks for bringing her back."

Yo momma's so ugly, that people at the circus pay money not to see her.

Yo momma's so ugly, her yellow teeth make cars slow down.

Yo momma's so ugly, even Rice Krispies won't talk to her!

Yo momma's so ugly, she could scare the moss off a rock!

Yo momma's so ugly, that when she goes to the therapist, he makes her lie on the couch face down.

Yo momma's so ugly, that it looks like she's been bobbing for French fries.

Yo momma's so ugly, that if she was a scarecrow, the corn would run away.

Yo momma's so ugly, that they didn't give her a costume when they cast her as the Elephant Man.

Yo momma's so ugly, that you have to tie a steak around her neck so the dog will play with her!

Yo momma's so ugly, that when she went to Taco Bell everyone ran for the border.

Yo momma's so ugly, that when she walked out of her house, the neighbors called animal control.

Yo momma's so ugly, that her shadow ran away from her.

Yo momma's so ugly, that when she walks into a bank, they turn off the surveillance cameras.

Yo momma's so ugly, that she entered an ugly, contest they said, "No professionals!"

MY YO

MOMMA

JOKES

Yo momma's so _____

that _____

_____

_____

_____.

Yo momma's so _____

that _____

_____

_____

_____.

Yo momma's so _____

that _____

_____

_____

_____.

Yo momma's so _____

that _____

_____

_____

_____.

Yo momma's so _____

that _____

_____

_____

_____.

Yo momma's so _____

that _____

_____

_____.

Yo momma's so _____

that _____

_____

_____

_____.

Yo momma's so _____

that _____

_____

_____

_____.

Yo momma's so _____

that _____

_____

_____

_____.

Yo momma's so _____

that _____

_____

_____

_____.

Yo momma's so _____

that _____

_____

_____

_____.

Yo momma's so _____

that _____

_____

_____

_____.

Yo momma's so _____

that _____

_____

_____

_____.

Yo momma's so _____

that _____

_____

_____

_____.

Yo momma's so _____

that _____

_____

_____

_____.

Yo momma's so _____

that _____

_____

_____

_____.

Yo momma's so _____

that _____

_____

_____

_____.

Yo momma's so _____

that _____

_____

_____

_____.

Yo momma's so _____

that _____

_____

_____

_____.

Yo momma's so _____

that _____

_____

_____

_____.

Yo momma's so _____

that _____

_____

_____

_____.

Yo momma's so _____

that _____

_____

_____

_____.

Yo momma's so _____

that _____

_____

_____

_____.

Yo momma's so _____

that _____

_____

_____

_____.

Made in the USA
Monee, IL
28 January 2023

26618811R00056